How and Why Science

Science

in

Fields

and

Forests

How and Why Science

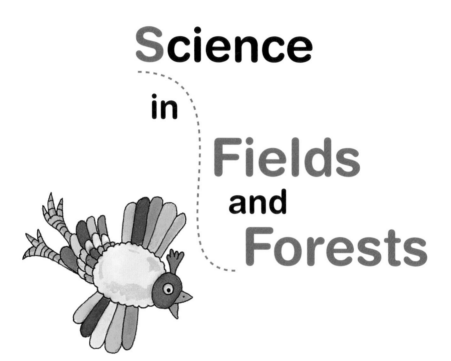

Science in Fields and Forests

World Book, Inc.

Chicago London Sydney Toronto

Acknowledgments

The publisher of Childcraft gratefully acknowledge the courtesy of illustrator John Sandford and the following photographers, agencies, and organizations for the illustrations in this volume. Credits should be read from left to right, top to bottom, on their respective pages. All illustrations are the exclusive property of the publisher of Childcraft unless names are marked with an asterisk (*).

8-9   Dan Rest
22-23   Larry Mulvehill, Photo Researchers*; Derrick Ditchburn, Visuals Unlimited*; Richard L. Carlton, Photo Researchers*
30-31   Robert Maier, Animals Animals*

World Book, Inc.
525 West Monroe
Chicago, IL 60661

Editors: Sharon Nowakowski, Melissa Tucker
Art Director: Wilma Stevens
Illustrator: John Sandford
Cover Design: Susan Newman
Cover Illustrator: Eileen Mueller Neill

Library of Congress Cataloging-in-Publication Data

Science in fields and forests.
    p. cm. -- (How and why science)
    Includes index.
    Summary: Introduces concepts of botany, ecology, and zoology through related experiments and activities that can be performed at home. Includes instructions for keeping a lab notebook.
    ISBN 0-7166-7110-7 (pbk.)
    1. Nature study--Juvenile literature. 2. Natural history--Experiments--Juvenile literature. [1. Nature study. 2. Natural history--Experiments. 3. Experiments.] I. World Book, Inc. II. Series.
QH51.S36   1998
508--dc21   98-15683

For information on other World Book products, call 1-800-255-1750, x2238, or visit us at our Web site at http://www.worldbook.com

Printed in Singapore

2 3 4 5 6 7 8 9 02 01 00 99

Introduction

When you picture scientists, do you imagine them working in big laboratories, surrounded by specialized equipment? Well, lots of scientists do, but many other scientists work outdoors in fields and forests. If you think like a scientist, you too can learn a lot from the plants, animals, and other living things outside your door. Just take the time to look, listen, and smell.

Science helps people answer questions such as, "Why do plants grow toward light? Why are some plants poisonous? How do animals communicate?" **Science in Fields and Forests** lets you be a scientist in your own backyard.

In this book, all kinds of scientists explain how they study the world. They'll show you how to have fun exploring on your own. Don't worry about not understanding unfamiliar words, they are defined in the margins. The **Aha!** feature highlights surprising science facts. When you are ready to try your skills, check out the **In Your Lab** sections.

Science is not just for professional botanists, ecologists, or zoologists. Science helps all of us understand the world around us.

How Do Plants GROW?

You and your friends eat fruits, vegetables, and other foods to grow up strong and healthy. But how do fruits, vegetables, and other plants grow? I happen to know because I'm a botanist. Plants use sunlight and simple ingredients such as water to make the food they need. However, plants can't cook, of course. When they make their own food, the process is called *photosynthesis* (FOH tuh SIHN thuh sihs). In photosynthesis, a plant uses the sun's energy to convert water and a gas called *carbon dioxide* (KAHR buhn dy AHK syd) into

A **botanist** (*BAHT uh nihst*) *is a scientist who studies plant life.*

sugar. Imagine not having to turn on an oven, ever! Well, it's not quite *that* easy.

Plants work constantly to gather what they need to make food. In fact, plants can actually move toward the things they need to make it. For example, vines in forests get to sunlight by climbing up trees. They cling to the tree trunks and then grow upward to reach the light. These movements that plants make are called tropisms (TROH pih zuhmz).

AHA!

Stroke the tip of a pea vine or a cucumber vine with a stick and watch the tip turn. You're seeing thigmotropism in action! *Thigmotropism* is the tendency of vines and some other plants to wrap around a support.

7

Tropisms are movements named for the signals that cause them. In Greek, **geo-** means "earth," **hydro-** means "water," **photos-** means "light," and **thigmo-** means "touch." **Tropism** comes from the Greek word **trope**, meaning "a turning."

A *tropism* is a plant's response to certain signals in the world around it. The movement of a plant toward light is called *phototropism*. Scientists call the plant's response to gravity *geotropism*. And different parts of a plant react in different ways to the pull of gravity. For example, the root of a plant responds to gravity by growing downward. This movement sends the root into the soil, where it can absorb water and minerals. The plant's stem also responds to gravity, but it reacts by growing upward instead of downward. This movement pushes the stem above the soil, where leaves can spread and absorb the sun's rays.

Have you ever seen a potted plant tipped on its side by accident? You may have noticed an upward bend in the plant's stem. Because of

geotropism, the stem started growing straight upward again—away from the pull of gravity. This made the stem crooked! You could not see the root, but it bent, too. Because of geotropism, it grew downward.

How did the root and the stem sense that they had been tilted off course? Like all living things, plants are made up of *cells*—tiny bits of living matter. Plants have special cells that sense gravity. They are found along a plant's stem and in the tip of its root. Each of these cells contains "sacks" of grains that sink to its lowest part.

As long as the plant is straight, the sacks lie at the bottom of the gravity-sensing cells. But when the plant is tilted, the sacks shift. Scientists think the shifting sacks start an uneven flow of chemicals that affect the plant's growth.

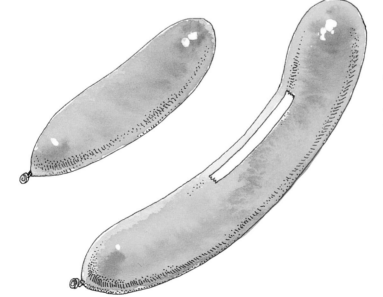

Blow up a balloon partway, then stick a piece of tape onto it. Continue blowing up the balloon and you will see that the tape lets one side expand, or grow, more than the other side. Just as the tape affects the way in which the balloon expands, chemicals in plants affect the direction in which roots and stems grow.

9

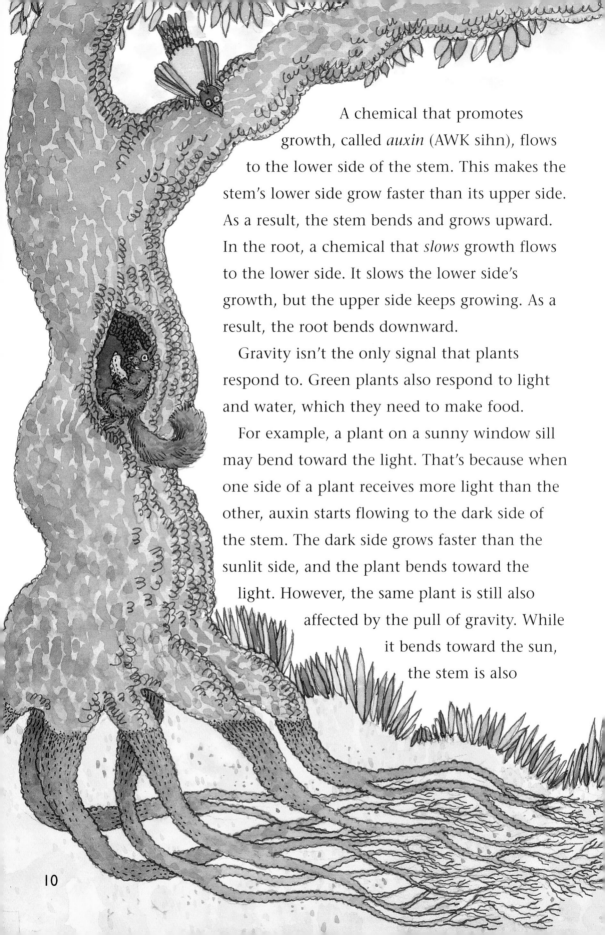

A chemical that promotes growth, called *auxin* (AWK sihn), flows to the lower side of the stem. This makes the stem's lower side grow faster than its upper side. As a result, the stem bends and grows upward. In the root, a chemical that *slows* growth flows to the lower side. It slows the lower side's growth, but the upper side keeps growing. As a result, the root bends downward.

Gravity isn't the only signal that plants respond to. Green plants also respond to light and water, which they need to make food.

For example, a plant on a sunny window sill may bend toward the light. That's because when one side of a plant receives more light than the other, auxin starts flowing to the dark side of the stem. The dark side grows faster than the sunlit side, and the plant bends toward the light. However, the same plant is still also affected by the pull of gravity. While it bends toward the sun, the stem is also growing upward. So the plant grows at an angle.

Although roots do not respond to light, they do grow toward water as well as gravity. Their movement toward water is known as *hydrotropism*. Hydrotropism sometimes pulls more strongly on roots than gravity. In very dry conditions, a root may grow sideways—toward an underground river, for instance. The roots of many desert trees spread out close to the surface to capture every drop of rainfall they can.

Plants don't look busy. They are so quiet, and they seem so still. But now you know that plants are constantly on the move, responding to signals that help them get the things they need to make their own food.

AHA!

Feeling lazy? Don't feel like getting up to get a glass of water? In the desert, the roots of the mesquite tree extend as deep as 263 feet (81 meters) just to get to water.

Seeking Light

Hmmmm . . . I wonder . . .
How strongly does a bean
plant seek light?
What if it doesn't get
any light?

GATHER TOOLS

- runner beans or dry pinto beans
- planting pots or cups
- potting soil
- empty shoe boxes or cracker boxes
- scissors
- black construction paper
- index cards as wide as the box
- tape

Set up and give it a try

1 Soak the beans overnight in water. Fill a pot with soil and plant a few beans. Keep the soil moist. Wait 5 to 7 days for a sprout.

2 Line the inside of the box with black paper. Cut the paper a little large. Then tape the paper in the box. Fold in the extra paper to help keep out light.

3 Cut an index card so that it is 1 1/2 inches (4 cm) shorter than the width of the box. Cover the card with black paper and tape it inside the box like a shelf. Cut a 1 1/2-inch hole near the top end of the box top.

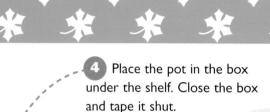

4 Place the pot in the box under the shelf. Close the box and tape it shut.

5 Place the box on a sunny window sill, with the hole facing the sun. Each day, open the box, observe the plant, and water it if it is dry. Then close the box.

Set up a control
Grow a bean plant in an identical box without a hole to see how it grows without light. Grow a bean plant on the same window sill without a box.

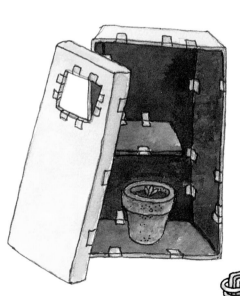

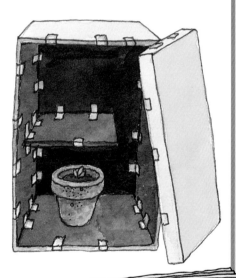

Try it again and again

• Use lamplight instead of sunlight. (Ask an adult for help to set it up safely.)

• Add another shelf.

• Use various kinds of plants.

Now, write it down

Keep notes on what happens daily for two weeks. Include when and how much you water your plants, how much sunlight is available, and how the plants look. Can you now answer the questions listed at the beginning of this lab? Do you have other questions? Keep testing.

Compare your notes with those on page 32.

Plant Poisons
Can Be Helpful

H. M. Lock here. I'm a biochemist on a mission. My job is to find useful substances in plants. This may surprise you, but some of the plants that help us the most are poisonous.

Scientists classify thousands of plants around the world as poisonous. A poisonous plant is one that contains a substance that can harm people or animals if they touch or swallow it. Even some house plants can be dangerous. For instance, the leaves and stems of the philodendron (fihl uh DEHN druhn) have crystals that burn your mouth and throat. Plant poisons can also produce problems such as skin rashes, stomachaches, and liver damage.

A **biochemist** (by oh KEHM ihst) is a scientist who studies the chemicals and chemical processes in living things.

Poisons are the plants' defense against plant-eaters. The poisons make these plants smell or taste bad, so many animals avoid them, including humans. After all, plants can't run away when in danger as animals do.

These defenses do not always work, however. Some animals don't mind the smell and taste of poisonous plants, and some of these animals aren't injured by plants that make people sick. For example, some rabbits produce a chemical in their bodies that changes certain plant poisons into harmless substances. Also, animals with four chambers in their stomach, such as deer, can eat bushels of poisonous plants with no ill effects.

Yuck!

15

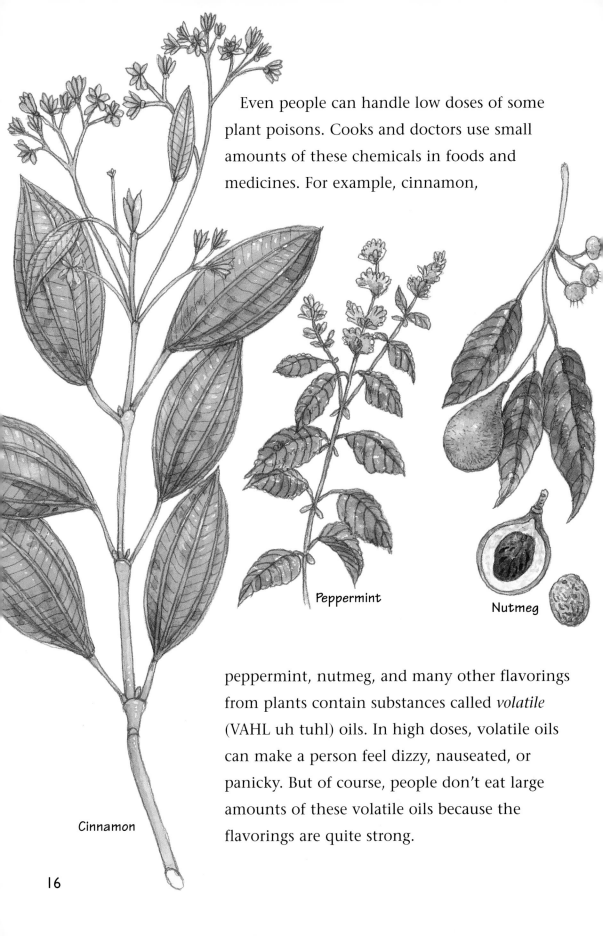

Even people can handle low doses of some plant poisons. Cooks and doctors use small amounts of these chemicals in foods and medicines. For example, cinnamon,

Peppermint

Nutmeg

peppermint, nutmeg, and many other flavorings from plants contain substances called *volatile* (VAHL uh tuhl) oils. In high doses, volatile oils can make a person feel dizzy, nauseated, or panicky. But of course, people don't eat large amounts of these volatile oils because the flavorings are quite strong.

Cinnamon

One group of plant poisons is known as *alkaloids* (AL kuh loydz). They are found in larkspur, glory lilies, belladonna, and many other garden plants. Eating these plants can cause numbness, vomiting, and even death. Yet doctors use alkaloids from glory lilies to treat serious diseases such as leprosy and cancer. And eye doctors drop an alkaloid from belladonna

The science called **pharmacognosy** *(FAHR muh KAHG nuh see) deals with the chemical substances in natural drugs. Some of these drugs come from poisons in plants.*

AHA!

Some poisons are found only in certain parts of a plant. The tuber of the potato—the part you bake, mash, or fry—is perfectly safe to eat, and so are the stems of rhubarb in rhubarb pie. But rhubarb leaves, and all the green parts of the potato plant, are poisonous.

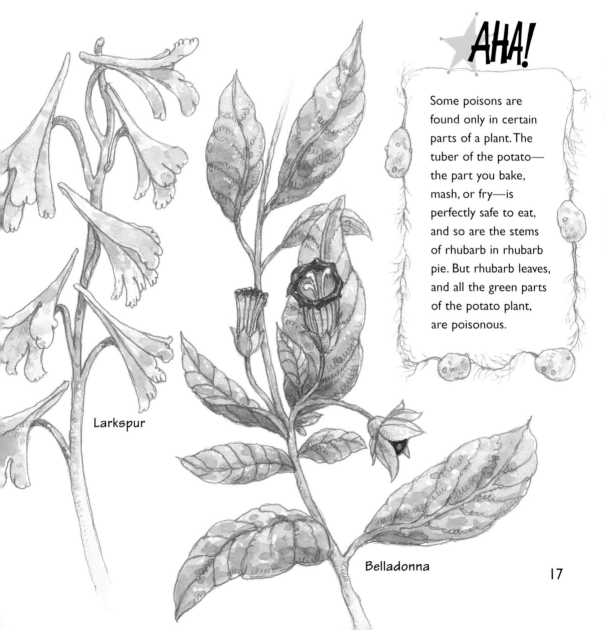

Larkspur

Belladonna

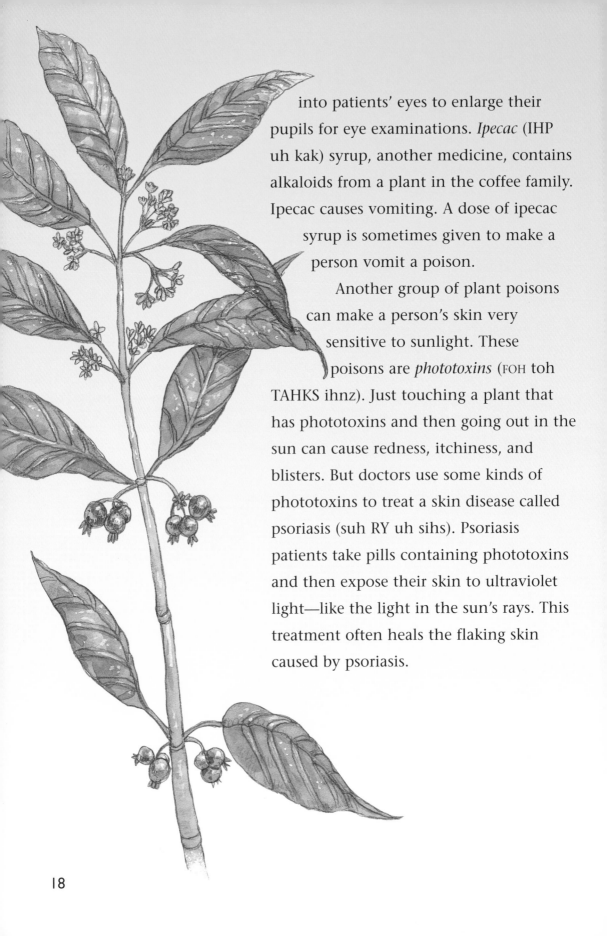

into patients' eyes to enlarge their pupils for eye examinations. *Ipecac* (IHP uh kak) syrup, another medicine, contains alkaloids from a plant in the coffee family. Ipecac causes vomiting. A dose of ipecac syrup is sometimes given to make a person vomit a poison.

Another group of plant poisons can make a person's skin very sensitive to sunlight. These poisons are *phototoxins* (FOH toh TAHKS ihnz). Just touching a plant that has phototoxins and then going out in the sun can cause redness, itchiness, and blisters. But doctors use some kinds of phototoxins to treat a skin disease called psoriasis (suh RY uh sihs). Psoriasis patients take pills containing phototoxins and then expose their skin to ultraviolet light—like the light in the sun's rays. This treatment often heals the flaking skin caused by psoriasis.

To be "plant smart," follow these tips:

✔ Learn which plants in your house and neighborhood are poisonous.

✔ Eat only what you have permission to eat. Remember, some parts of a plant may be poisonous even though you can eat other parts.

✔ Keep babies and pets away from house plants.

✔ Stay away from burning plants. Breathing in their smoke may be bad for you. Smoke from burning poison ivy, for example, is especially dangerous.

✔ When cooking over a campfire, don't roast hot dogs or other foods on branches from poisonous plants or plants you don't know are safe.

✔ Make sure your family's first-aid kit has instructions for treating a poison victim.

✔ Know the phone number of your local poison control center or put the number by your home telephones.

An Outdoor Habitat

How well do you know your nearest neighbors, the plants and animals in the yard, garden, or park near your house? I ask because I'm an ecologist. My name is Barry E. Cology, and I study plants and animals everywhere I can, even in my own backyard. My backyard is a habitat for many living things. A *habitat* is the area of land, air, or water—or all these places—where a living thing dwells.

You say you want to know more about *your* neighbors? Well, I'll share my science secrets so you can see how ecologists study habitats.

First, an ecologist needs to mark off a small area of the habitat to be explored. Just as nobody can examine all of Earth at once, I can't closely examine all of my backyard at once. So, I set up a transect and a quadrat (KWAH druht). It's easier than it sounds.

To make a transect, I drive a *stake,* or pointed stick, into the ground. Next, I walk 10 feet (3 m) and put in another stake. Then I connect the stakes with string. This straight string above the ground is my *transect*. Be careful not to trip!

Next, I make a quadrat, which can look like a pie or a checkerboard. For example, a square *quadrat* is a 3-foot (about 1-m) square made of wood, screws, string, and tacks that form 16 smaller squares. I toss the quadrat under the transect. Now I have marked off an area of my yard that I can easily explore.

When I study my neighbors, I always bring along a backpack with graph paper, colored pencils, a magnifying glass, and *field guides* (illustrated books about wildlife). On the graph paper, I draw straight lines to represent the transect. Each square stands for some number of inches or centimeters on the transect.

AHA!

In the United States, it's illegal to kill or capture endangered butterfly species, such as the Schaus swallowtail and the San Bruno elfin. International laws make capturing butterflies illegal in other countries, too. So now, butterfly enthusiasts and butterfly specialists, *lepidopterists (lehp uh DAHP tuhr ihsts)*, plant flowers to attract butterflies. Then they can observe and photograph the lovely creatures up close, without having to capture or kill them.

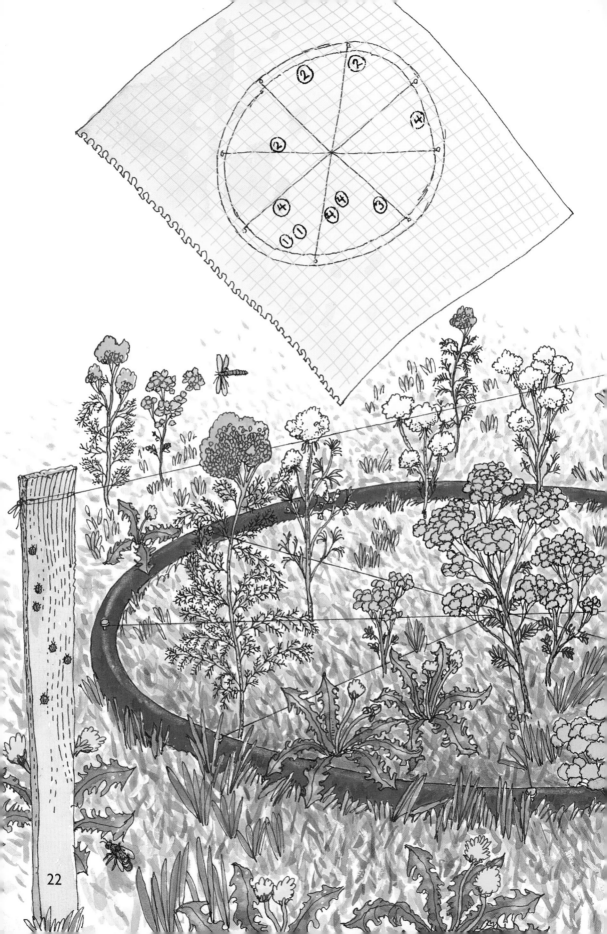

Field Guide

Dandelion

Queen Anne's lace

Tansy

Try your skill at identifying wildflowers. Can you match Barry's wildflower sketches to photos in this field guide?
answers on page 32

I sketch plants that lie under the transect. Then I sketch the insects that live on the plants. On another sheet of graph paper, I draw a map of the quadrat.

On my maps, I label the plants and animals I know. To identify unfamiliar ones, I look for clues. Take wildflowers, for example. Their leaves and petals are usually arranged in set patterns. When I find a wildflower, I note its color. I carefully sketch its leaf and petal patterns. Then I compare my sketch with pictures in a field guide. Usually I find a match.

I write down more than just names, though. I also record the *population* (number) of each kind of living thing within the quadrat. And I describe differences in the soil. Later, I compare this information to other areas in my yard.

The more information I collect, the more I can find out about the plants and animals that live in that habitat. Humans usually feel climate conditions 3 feet or more above the ground. But plants and animals that live at ground level may experience a different climate, and animals in the trees can experience yet other climates. These climates that exist in small parts of a habitat are called *microclimates*. For example, rocks shade and cool parts of the ground, and trees block winds.

To study microclimates, I make a temperature pole. I start with an old broomstick whittled to a point. I drive the point into the ground along the transect. Then I tie three cardboard tubes to the broomstick— one at ground level, one a foot (30 cm) high, and one at 3 feet. Three thermometers are tied so that one falls inside each tube. The tubes shield the thermometers from the sun. I check the thermometers several times a day and record the temperatures on my transect map.

Finally, I lie on the ground and just watch the wildlife along the transect and in the quadrats. I try to look at the habitat through the eyes of a small creature. I imagine being a butterfly. Fluttering in the air, I watch bees sucking nectar and look for a flower for myself. I spot a beetle nibbling petals, aphids sipping sap, and a wasp chewing pollen. The bee lands on a blossom and prepares to sip nectar. Suddenly, a hungry yellow crab spider sidles into view and the bee is off again.

Web-Weaver Habitats

Hmmmm . . . I wonder . . .
Where do spiders in my backyard
habitat weave their webs?
Are all webs the same?
Are the locations of different webs
alike in any way?

Caution! Don't touch or play with any spiders that you find. Most spiders do not harm humans, but some spider bites are painful, and a few are even dangerous.

GATHER TOOLS

- colored pencils
- drawing paper
- a hard book or clipboard to put paper on when writing

IMPORTANT: Get an adult's permission before doing this activity.

Set up and give it a try

1. Visit your backyard or a park (ask permission first). Draw a diagram of the area on a sheet of plain paper. Include trees, bushes, walls, tables, and play equipment. Then search for spider webs. Check under slides, steps, and ladders, as well as in low and high corners of supporting bars and beams.

2. Each time you find a web, mark its location on your diagram by writing a number (start with #1 and go up). Copy that number on a separate sheet of paper. Next to the number, sketch the web. Write a description of the web's location using words such as *shady*, *sunny*, *dry*, *damp*, *hidden*, or *exposed*.

Tangled web

Orb web

3 Identify each web's type by comparing it with the web types shown here.

Funnel web

Sheet web

Set up a control

Search for webs in other yards or parks.

Try it again and again

- Be sure to go web searching at a site both on a sunny day and then again after a rain or storm.

- Map your basement, attic, or garage and locate webs there.

Now, write it down

Compare your descriptions of the webs you found. Are they all the same? Are they all found in the same type of location? What can you conclude about spider habitats?

Compare your notes with those on page 32.

What's That Squirrel Saying?

A **zoologist** (zoh AHL uh jihst) is a scientist who studies all aspects of animal life.

Pheromone (FEHR uh mohn) is a chemical substance released by many kinds of animals to communicate with other members of their species.

Hello! Can you stay for a chat? I love to communicate. As a zoologist, I enjoy seeing how animals communicate. At first, I admit, their "conversations" didn't seem much like ours. But then I learned that animals communicate through sounds, movements, and scents called pheromones. I only had to figure out what these things meant!

Most animals don't think about what they want to communicate. Instead, they act largely by instinct. In other words, they behave in ways

28

that they have inherited from their parents and grandparents. These ways help them survive. For example, a ground squirrel whistles when it sees an animal that hunts it, the hawk, circling above. The whistle is a medium-pitched sound, a difficult sound to locate. It doesn't reveal the squirrel's position. But other squirrels hear the warning, and they scramble to their burrows.

When a badger slinks nearby, the same ground squirrel chatters an alarm. The chatter is a mixture of low- and high-pitched sounds. These sounds are easier to locate than medium-pitched ones. As a result, other ground squirrels know where the badger is. They run and hide. As the badger passes each hiding place, another squirrel chatters, revealing the badger's new location. This

Instinct (IHN stingkt) is something a person or animal does or knows without having to learn it. For example, babies don't have to learn to smile when they are happy. They do it because of instinct.

A ground squirrel whistles to signal that a hawk is circling above.

behavior shows how animals cooperate to survive. The frustrated badger gives up and goes away hungry.

The new science of **bioacoustics** *(BY oh uh KOOS tihks) studies the sounds that animals make.*

Prairie dogs, cousins of ground squirrels, are great communicators, too. When two prairie dogs meet, they sniff each other's faces. They identify relatives by their scents. If the prairie dogs are family members, they may "kiss" again. If their scents are unfamiliar, they chatter and chase each other around.

A deer makes relatively little noise, but it communicates in other ways. For example, when a *buck* (male deer) looks for a mate, he may paw the ground, urinate, and deposit a

An axis deer leaves his scent on branches to mark his territory.

A rabbit warns other rabbits of danger by thumping the ground.

AHA!

Wolves communicate with facial expressions— just like you do. When you're happy, you smile. When a wolf is happy, its tongue hangs out loosely and its ears point forward. But if a wolf wrinkles its nose, shows its teeth, and perks its ears up straight—watch out! It's ready to fight.

pheromone, or scent, produced between his toes. This scent attracts nearby *does* (dohz) (female deer). A buck also leaves a scent when he rubs his forehead against tree branches. This scent warns other bucks to stay off his territory.

Rabbits release pheromones to mark their territory. When they sense danger, rabbits warn others by thumping the ground with their hind feet. Then they hop away fast, looking for cover.

Do you want to know what animals have to say? Then look, listen, and smell when they come near. Maybe you will learn something.

Think Safety!

While science is fun, it's not exactly play. So it's time to talk safety. When you are doing experiments, always remember the rule, "Safety first." Help prevent accidents in the following ways:

- Before you begin a lab, read all instructions carefully. If you don't fully understand an instruction, ask a grown-up for help.

- Avoid spills, but just in case, line your work area with old newspapers before starting an experiment.

- While doing an experiment, do not eat or drink anything. Never, never put substances in your mouth.

- Keep first-aid supplies handy. Make sure you know where they are.

- If in doubt, don't do it. Taking chances can harm you or others.

- Ask a grown-up for help whenever you use chemicals, heat, sharp objects, or anything else that can hurt you.

- When you work with chemicals or flames, always wear safety goggles to protect your eyes.

- Don't fool around—it can be dangerous! Have fun, but treat your science experiments seriously.

Answers & Lab Notes

Answers

page 23 *Barry's field guide and drawings*
Barry's sketch labeled I matches the dandelion in the field guide. His wildflower labeled 2 is Queen Anne's lace. Barry's sketch labeled 4 is a tansy. Don't be fooled by sketch number 3; it isn't in the field guide!

Lab Notes

Here are some notes and findings you may have made when doing the labs presented in this book. There aren't any right or wrong notes. In fact, you probably made many observations different from the ones given here. That's okay. What can you conclude from them? If a lab didn't turn out the way you thought it would, that's okay too. Do you know why it didn't? If not, go back and find out. After doing a lab, did you come up with more questions, different from the ones you had when you started? If you did, good. Grab your journal and your science kit and start looking for more answers!

pages 12-13 *Seeking Light*

After several days or weeks, there are distinct differences in the way the main plant and the control plants look. In the maze, the plant bends toward the hole, the light source. The plant without any light begins to wilt, turns brown, and eventually dies.

pages 26-27 *Web-Weaver Habitats*

Spiders weave webs in different and strange places. Sheet webs and funnel webs are generally found close to the ground. Funnel webs are often built in tall grass or under rocks or logs. Sheet webs are often found between blades of grass or branches of shrubs or trees, even along the edges of steams and lakes. Orb webs, the most complicated webs of all, hang in open areas, often between tree branches or flower stems. Not typically found in shaded areas, orb webs are frequently seen in gardens, meadows, and along roadsides. Tangled webs are often in dark corners, especially in homes. These webs are attached to a support, such as the corner of a ceiling. Dusty, dirty old tangled webs are called cobwebs.